D0948461

The
Reduced History of
RUGBY

First published in 2005 by
André Deutsch Ltd
An imprint of the
Carlton Publishing Group
20 Mortimer Street
London W1T 3JW

Copyright © André Deutsch Ltd 2005

A CIP catalogue record for this book
is available from the British Library

ISBN 0 23300 122 0

Printed in Singapore

Words: Iain Spragg
Editor: Justyn Barnes
Editorial Consultant: Aubrey Ganguly
Illustrations: Tony Husband
Art Director/Jacket Design: Olly Smee
Photoshop/Design: Martin Dickson
Production: Lisa French
Commissioning Editor: Martin Corteel

The
Reduced History of
RUGBY

The oval-shaped story of the Union game squeezed into 80 minutes

Iain Spragg Illustrations by Tony Husband

ANDRE
DEUTSCH

This book is dedicated to everyone who seeks the meaning of life, rugby and John Inverdale...

INTRODUCTION

Rugby, eh? Who'd have thought a game played with an odd-shaped ball, where you have to pass backwards to go forwards and you may often find yourself buried under a heap of sweating, heaving men could be so much fun. But it is, and people have enjoyed it ever since a weird schoolkid called William picked up a football and ran with it way back in 1823.

And what an aftershave-supping (not so smart, Colin...), scrotum-ripping (ouch, Wayne Shelford), leg-shaving (ooh, Gavin) 180-odd years it's been. But how could we possibly cram it all into one book – especially, a book as perfectly formed, but, let's face it, small, as this one?

Luckily, dear reader, that was our problem, not yours. We scoured parchments, newspapers and books as thick as the average prop forward so you don't have to.

Instead, sit back, relax and enjoy (very) abbreviated highlights from Rugby Union's historic history, freshly squeezed into 80 minutes (plus extra time!). Let's, er, ruck!

KICK-OFF

Weird kid William invents rugger

Cheating schoolboy creates a whole new ball game

Rugby Union (or a legalised punch-up with a couple of pints afterwards) began life way back in 1823 at Rugby School when William Webb Ellis realised he was sick and tired of football (or legalised prancing about and a couple of white wine spritzers afterwards) and decided to pick up the ball during a game and run with it.

This one act of shame-faced schoolboy cheating, or "fine disregard for the rules" as someone more poetically put it at the time, was to spawn a global sport played by millions of allegedly sane people.

Webb Ellis, who was not the most popular of the chaps at school by all accounts (especially among the football fans), went on to take holy orders (and what a conversion that was) and died in Paris, where he is buried, in 1872.

'That's detention for you my lad..."

Hacked off!

Anarchy reigns in the lawless early afternoons of rugby history

The early rules of rugby were pretty vague and most teams just decided to make their own up as they went along. This was a bit of a problem, not least because no-one ever knew if the other side was cheating.

By the 1840s, however, the tide was turning and like a new sheriff in a lawless Wild West town, the authorities were trying to impose order. Take Rugby School's attempt to clear a few important points up:

'Hacking is permitted, but not above the knee. Holding a player carrying the ball is permitted, but passing with the hands is banned. And if no decision is reached after five afternoons, play, a match will be declared a draw.'

Simple rules for a simpler time.

They say rugby is a religion in Wales – which is fitting since it was actually a man of the cloth who exported the game from England to the Principality back in the 1850.

The man in question was the Reverend Rowland Williams, who landed a job as deputy headmaster of St David's College in Lampeter, and soon began, um, preaching the virtues of the game to the locals.

In fact, the Welsh didn't need much convincing and, since it gave them the opportunity to put one over on the English, rugby soon became the national obsession. As well as Shirley Bassey, obviously. Oh, and hating the English.

Wales now boasts hundreds of clubs, a lovely new stadium in Cardiff with a roof thingy and more players called Jones than you could ever possibly hope to keep up with.

New balls, please...

Big lungs Gilbert blows up pig's bladders

Rugby is a game played by men with funny-shaped balls and they didn't come much funnier than the balls from the sport's early days in the 1850s, which varied wildly in shape, size and weight.

Step forward enterprising bright spark William Gilbert, a boot- and shoe-maker who worked for Rugby School. Gilbert hit upon the idea of manufacturing a standard leather oval ball inflated with a pig's bladder.

Gilbert, described by his contemporaries as "a wonder of lung strength who blew even the big match balls up tight", displayed the game's first commercially produced ball at the London Exhibition in 1851. His innovation was such a hit that he soon abandoned cobbling (shoes, not paving stones) and went into ball manufacturing full-time.

5 Flamingos... Gypsies... Mohicans!
Freaky clubs form Rugby Football Union after lunch

The Rugby Football Union (or RFU) is an old and venerable institution and its committee members' efforts to keep the gin industry in rude health should never be underestimated.

Some might think the corridors of power at Twickenham slightly dusty and old-fashioned but such critics obviously know little about the origins of the Union. Founded in 1871 after a hearty (and not entirely liquid) lunch at the Pall Mall restaurant, the RFU was established by an array of bizarrely named clubs that put to shame the unimaginative, corporate-branded teams of today. Among the clubs represented at the meeting were the Flamingos, Gipsies, Wimbledon Hornets, Marlborough Nomads and, of course, Mohicans.

20-a-side rugger!
Edinburgh stages first-ever international in 1871

The animosity between the English and the Scots is as old as most of the jokes in this book, so it is perhaps fitting that these two nations were the first ever to contest an international match. After all, by 1871 there hadn't been an Anglo-Scottish dust-up (military or otherwise) for what seemed like ages and everyone was, frankly, itching for a bit of cross-border confrontation.

The game was held at Raeburn Place in Edinburgh. No-one seemed to notice or care, however, that both sides had 20 men in their starting line-ups (told you they made the rules up as they went along...) and Scotland emerged from a packed pitch as winners by a goal and a try to one try.

It was not until 1877 that everyone decided 15-a-side would do just fine, thank you very much.

Traders pass rugby to the French

Alcohol lubricates flow of rugby across the Channel

There is something very suspicious about the fact France embraced rugby in the same year the game's founding figure – William Webb Ellis – died. It's even more strange that Rugby School's most famous pupil is buried in France. Hmm, all in all, it makes the JFK shooting look like an open and shut case...

Anyway, France caught the rugby bug in 1872 when British wine merchants in Le Havre decided to take a break from getting smashed and chasing the local girls and set up a rugby club in the port town. The French took to rugby like ducks to force-feeding and within five years the game had taken hold in Paris and the rest of the country. In 1885, a French side toured Britain for the first time and by 1920 the Fédération de France Rugby was formed.

Mange tout, mes amis!

Stolen ball stops play!

1877 West Wales Challenge Cup final between Cardiff and Llanelli abandoned after a spectator half-inches the match ball (there were no spares in those days…)

POLICE REPORT

Name	PC J.P.R. Williams-Edwards-Jenkins
Date	One day in 1877
Incident	Theft of rugby ball

I proceeded to the ground from an easterly direction and arrived at 3.37 pm. Upon my arrival, I was greeted by much wretched wailing from members of the crowd, who assured me they were not, in fact, the male voice choir. I began my investigations forthwith and soon discovered a shocking tale of theft and opportunism. It quickly transpired that the missing ball was indeed still missing and I would go as far as to say it was, in fact, not there. I inquired in which direction the suspect had perambulated following the said incident and was informed through the medium of pointing fingers that he had, and I quote, "legged it that way". I attempted to apprehend the suspect but could not do so because he wasn't there and returned to the station for a cup of tea. And a biscuit.

Let there be light
Floodlights are introduced to rugby

The first recorded rugby match played under
floodlights took place in October 1878 when
Broughton entertained Swinton at their Yew Street
ground in Salford. The illumination was supplied by
lights suspended from 30-foot poles in each corner,
and 10,000 crammed into the ground to witness the
spectacle – the home side beating their visitors by two
goals, three tries and three touchdowns to nil.

Butcher Ned gives rugger the chop!

Purveyor of fine meats (and haggis) invents game with quite literally less players

Seven-a-side rugby (well, you couldn't have seven-and-a-half-a-side, could you?) was invented by a Scottish butcher by the name of Ned Haig in 1883.

A member of the Melrose club, Haig came up with the idea for the shortened form of the game when a cash crisis gripped his beloved club and they were looking for ways to raise some dosh quickly.

Haig initially suggested a drive-through haggis emporium, but dropped the idea when someone quite reasonably pointed out none of them had cars. Instead, he opted for a seven-a-side rugby festival.

"Want of money made us rack our brains as to what was to be done to keep the club from going to the wall," Haig said after his brainwave. "The idea struck me that a tournament might prove attractive but as it was hopeless to think of having several games in one afternoon with fifteen players on each side, so the teams were reduced to seven men."

Nice going, Ned!

Refs can go whistle

Officials given new (and very irritating) equipment in 1883

The most common complaint from referees in the early days of the game was the fact that everyone complained about them all the time. Some things, it seems, never change.

The second was the tendency to get nasty sore throats from all the shouting they had to do at naughty players. The problem of course was that rugby's whistle-blowers didn't actually have any whistles and every decision had to be barked out to the players with as many decibels as the poor souls could muster.

But that all changed in 1883 when they were finally equipped with whistles. Some would say they've been making up for lost time ever since...

Capital clash

Irish rugby gets new home

The oldest international venue in rugby history is Lansdowne Road in Dublin, which staged its first Test match in 1884 between Ireland and England.

Amazingly, some of the Ireland fans actually made it out of the pubs in time to see the game and witness the English scrape a narrow win. Dublin's pubs and bars have been raking it in ever since.

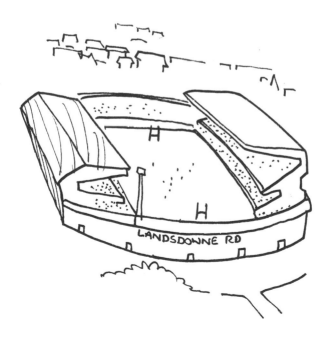

What's the point?

For years, games were decided by a scoring system that didn't actually have a system for scoring...

Rather than awarding points for scores, early games were decided by the number of goals, tries and penalties each team scored (think of it as a more physical version of Top Trumps) and a winner was somehow declared.

That all changed, however, in 1886 when the International Board decided a proper points-scoring system that you didn't need a degree to work out would be a jolly good idea. They opted for a point for a try and two for a conversion but also decreed a match could only be decided if a team scored a converted try.

Converting tries was easier said than done in those days because the rugby posts were not what you could call uniform. In fact, early uprights were pretty much whatever size and shape the local carpenter felt he could manage and it wasn't until the early twentieth century they took on their standard "H" design and dimensions – the crossbar 3 metres (10 feet) from the ground and the posts 5.6 metres (18 feet) apart.

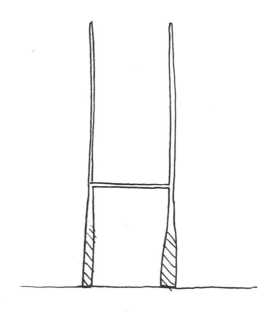

Lions roar Down Under

Famous tourists make maiden voyage

The first-ever British & Irish Lions squad set off for Australia and New Zealand in 1888, when dragons still ruled the world and policeman were over 18 and walked the beat.

The tour was a controversial one because the Rugby Football Union refused to recognise it (maybe it was wearing a disguise), and the 22 players, drawn mainly from England and Scotland, who headed Down Under were not awarded caps for the "internationals" on the trip.

The Lions played a total of 53 games but the sneaky Aussies insisted 18 of the games should be Australian Rules ... which is a different game. The Lions agreed, which was a bit daft really because they lost 11 of them.

Kiwis sail away after marathon tour of British Isles

Modern players can often be heard moaning about burnout and fatigue (and, increasingly, the exorbitant price of firm-hold hair gel), but they're pampered prima donnas compared to the early and considerably more durable pioneers of the game.

Take the New Zealand Maoris side who broke new ground on their 1888 tour to dear old Blighty. Now these Kiwis could even teach evergreen pop star/tantric sexpert Sting a thing or two about, ahem, staying power, playing an incredible 74 games in 18 months before they finally got sick and tired of the British weather and decided to jump on a ship heading home.

Overworked refs get helping hand
Touch judges take their bow

There's an old saying about rugby referees ... but sadly the obscenity laws mean it can't be repeated here. Suffice to say the official's visual capabilities and his parents' marital status both feature prominently and you probably wouldn't want your 10-year-old repeating it around the house when you've got visitors.

Which is all a little harsh on the game's fine and upstanding whistle-blowers when you consider it wasn't until 1889 that the powers-that-be thought they could do with some help and introduced touch judges for international clashes.

Everyone welcomed the move. The crowds loved it (they now had three people to scream at), the players were happy (ditto) and the referees themselves had someone to share a cuppa with in the changing room. Job done.

The great divide

Greedy northerners cause huge row and rugby league is born

The most famous sporting split before Dean realised he really could do a lot better than Torvill, the birth of the silly 13-a-side game called Rugby League caused so much controversy that even today devotees of Union and League often refuse to speak to each other at social gatherings.

It all started in 1893 when a group of northern clubs decided it really was high time to compensate their players for lost earnings while on club duty, an idea which went down like a stripper at a children's tea party with their southern counterparts.

Much kicking of whippets and jellying of eels ensued as the two camps argued about the idea of

"broken time payments" (surely they meant professionalism?) until 22 clubs from Yorkshire and Lancashire said enough was enough at a meeting in Huddersfield in 1895 and formed the Northern Union, which was to become the Rugby League.

The southern clubs immediately took the rebel 22 off their Christmas card list, had another gin and tonic and decided to tell anyone who would listen that they never really liked them in the first place.

Apparently, Rugby League is still played to this very day in front of crowds which have been known to reach double figures...

Monkey business

Welsh cause uproar in 1896 with unusual retirement gift

Rugby's almost religious fervour for amateurism was severely put to the test in the late nineteenth century when bigwigs in Wales decided to give one of their players a suspiciously generous leaving present.

The man in question was one Arthur "Monkey" Gould – he got his nickname after winning the Welsh Schoolboys tree-climbing contest three years running (probably) – and the gift was a house. To be fair, it was actually Gould's house, which the Welsh RFU generously decided to buy for him when he announced his international retirement after winning 27 caps for his country.

Now it didn't need Sherlock Holmes to work out this wasn't exactly in the spirit of amateurism (Holmes was gutted – he needed the work), and the Ireland and Scotland RFUs took it particularly badly, sulking like jilted teenagers and refusing to play Wales for the next three years. So there.

19 Your number's up

Players' shirts finally get numbered

Unfortunately, the introduction of shirt numbers in 1897 meant the players were forced to learn to count to at least 15 to take full advantage of the innovation. For many (particularly the forwards) it proved a bridge too far. If only Carol Vorderman's great, great, great granny had been around to help...

Schoolboy selection thwarted

Scots go for youth ... but headmaster scuppers plans

If you're good enough, you're old enough was obviously an adage the Scottish selectors took to heart in 1903 when they retired to the bar in time-honoured tradition to pick a team to play Wales in Edinburgh. After a few (too many) malts, they thought it would be a jolly wheeze to pick a 15-year-old schoolboy by the name of Kenneth MacLeod for the game.

However their plans (which even struck them as a wee bit silly when they sobered up) were thrown into disarray when MacLeod's headmaster at Fettes College told them his young protégé was far too busy with his homework, reading the *Beano* and worrying about puberty for this ridiculous rugby lark. Two years later, the sozzled selectors tried again but the school was still having none it.

MacLeod finally went on to study at Cambridge and, away from the clutches of the Fettes headmaster and the threat of detention, made his Scotland debut against the All Blacks, three months short of his 18th birthday. MacLeod went on to win 10 caps before hanging up his boots ... aged 20!

Yellow Yanks

In 1905, US President Theodore Roosevelt decides rugger's for the chop

Bloody Americans, eh? You (okay, William Webb Ellis to be precise) invent a perfectly good sport (give or take the odd concussion and maiming) and they still have to go and mess about with it.

It all started at the turn of the twentieth century when President Roosevelt watched a game between sides from Sarthmore and Pennsylvania universities and nearly choked on his pretzel (which seems to be an occupational hazard for American leaders). The sensitive Prez was so appalled by the levels of violence he witnessed (what exactly did he expect?) that he threatened to ban the game unless something was done to stop this obvious threat to national security.

Everyone fell into line, of course, and the faint-hearted Yanks began developing a ridiculous sport called American Football, complete with girly padding, helmets and incessant advertising breaks.

Billy's cabbage patch

Today, Twickenham is the spiritual home of rugby, but in 1907 it was the home to a muddy field full of cabbages ... and we're not talking about front-row forwards

Back at the start of the early nineteenth century, England did not have a permanent base until RFU committee member Billy Williams decided a 10-acre south London plot would make an ideal spot to build a new stadium.

Williams managed to buy the land in Twickenham for the princely sum of £5,573 – which was a lot of pennies in those days – and the England team were nomads no more.

The development of the site – which affectionately (but not very imaginatively) became known as "Billy Williams' Cabbage Patch" – followed soon after and three years later England played their first game at their new home, beating Wales 11–6.

What happened to all the displaced cabbages remains a mystery...

Dozy Bert gets lost in a peasouper

Even the most ardent fan would admit not all rugby players are Mensa candidates but full-back Bert Winfield really took the dunce's hat and ran with it in 1908 when Wales played England in Bristol.

It was a match badly affected by the West Country fog and both sides were more than happy to retreat to the warmth of their dressing rooms when the final whistle blew.

Back inside, however, 14 of the Welsh boys eventually realised they were missing one of their number – it was in the days before silly distractions like substitutes – and began a search for their missing-in-action team-mate. The bizarre game of hide-and-seek culminated in dozy Bert being found still out on the pitch, peering hopefully into the fog and claiming he thought the game was still being played.

Winfield went on to enjoy a long and successful career as a referee. Probably.

24 Welsh wonders

Championship witnesses first clean sweep

The Welsh teams of the 1970s are rightly revered in the Principality (almost as much as Tom Jones's chest hair) but there is also a special place in the fans' hearts for the side of 1908 who became the first Home Nations country to win the Grand Slam.

Captained by our old friend Bert Winfield (see No. 23), Wales beat England 28–18, Scotland 6–5 and Ireland 11–5 (France hadn't been invited into the competition yet) to record their historic clean sweep and cause daffodil- and sheep-throwing joy in the Valleys.

The star of the show was winger Reggie Gibbs, who scored six tries, and the Welsh love affair with rugby was well and truly consummated.

The French love of food is legendary but in the case of international player Gaston Vareilles it also proved to be his downfall.

Picked to play against Scotland in Paris in 1911, Vareilles caught a train to the French capital for the game but when it made a brief, unscheduled stop outside the city, the peckish winger hopped off for a bite to eat.

Vareilles must have been fumbling around for his loose francs because, by the time he finally managed to buy his baguette, his train had pulled out of the station without him and he was stranded.

The hapless winger quickly made alternative travel arrangements but, even though he made it to the ground before kick-off, he was told a replacement had already been found and, frankly, he could go somewhere quiet and finish his precious sandwich for all they cared. France narrowly won the game and guzzling Gaston never played for his country again.

Rugby players volunteered in their thousands for both of the World Wars, so it was no great surprise that in 1915 England and Northampton star Edgar Mobbs signalled to his First World War troops that it was time to go over the top by kicking a rugby ball into no man's land.

Mobbs had initially been rejected by the army for being too old but formed his own unit of sporting friends called "Mobbs Own" and fought for his country. He was killed at Passchendaele in 1917, leading a charge on a machine gun post, and was posthumously awarded the Distinguished Service Order medal.

Legendary BBC commentator Bill McLaren (see No. 30) might often have referred to players "charging around like an angry rhinoceros" but in the tragic case of England and Lions forward Denys Dobson that vision became all too real.

A member of the Great Britain tour of New Zealand and Australia in 1904 (where, incidentally, he became the first international player sent from the field for "obscene language"), Dobbo later emigrated to Malawi in central Africa to run a farm after he hung up his boots in 1916.

Sadly, it proved to be an ill-fated venture for Dobbo who was subsequently trampled to death by a charging rhino.

28 WW invents the scrum...

...and it's cauliflower ears all round!

In 1920, England captain Wavell Wakefield introduced the idea of players having specialist positions in the forwards, giving birth to the modern, unfathomable and frequently violent ritual known as the scrum.

Little could WW have realised at the time, however, that his innovation would lead to the most gruesome and mysterious of all sporting injuries – the cauliflower ear.

An ugly, menacing-looking inflammation that has made countless cameo

appearances in films such as *Evil Dead* and a *Nightmare on Elm Street*, the dreaded "colly" can strike a player at any time without warning and force normal people to flee in terror after just one glimpse at the terrible affliction.

Many players resort to syringing to temporarily escape the curse but, despite medical science making huge leaps and bounds in this area, there remains no known cure.

Dave or Dafydd?

Welsh bloke becomes England's record-breaking skipper

The rugby rivalry between England and Wales is about as friendly as a get-together between Yoko Ono and Paul McCartney. As one Englishman once put it: "The relationship between the Welsh and the English is based on trust and understanding. They don't trust us and we don't understand them."

But don't think there haven't been examples of cross-border generosity over the years.

Take the case of William "Dave" Davies, who was appointed England captain in 1921 and led the side 11 times. Under his leadership, the team won 10 and drew one of their fixtures, making him statistically the most successful England skipper of all time.

Funny thing is, Davies was actually born in Wales.

Bill McLaren was born in the Scottish border town of Hawick in 1923 and rugby commentary was never to be quite the same again. Known as the "voice of rugby", Macca's dulcet tones on the BBC became synonymous with the game until his retirement in 2002. Here we present a handy translation guide for some of the great man's most famous (and occasionally indecipherable) turns of phrase...

"He's got scuttling pace, like a kind of flying Charlie Chaplin" – The player is deceptively fast.

"A bit of hanky-panky in the lineout" – A minor infringement by one, possibly two of the lineout forwards.

"He's like a starving whippet" – The player chased down the ball with real conviction.

"The referee'll need to be on his toes at this scrum; they get up to all sorts of shenanigans in there" – Never, ever trust a prop forward.

"A lovely little shilly-shally there" – The player executed a deft sidestep.

"Jiggery pokery!" – He just blatantly and repeatedly punched his opposite number, but I've got to be seen to be neutral.

"That could have made it 10–3 and there's a subtle difference between that and 7–3" – I've completely lost the plot.

Golden Yanks

Americans reign supreme as Olympic champs

Theodore Roosevelt may not have been a big fan of rugby (see No. 21) but who cares what a man whose nickname was "Teddy" thinks anyway. Fortunately Roosevelt's Grand Canyon-sized yellow streak didn't stop America sending a team to the 1924 Olympic Games in Paris ... and winning gold!

The States team was stuffed full of students from Stanford University. Luckily for them, their games started late in the afternoon, so they just managed to get out of bed in time for kick-off.

The US overcame Romania in the semi-final before taking on and beating the hosts France, who instantly demanded the Yanks give back the Statue of Liberty.

Rugby was axed from the 1928 Games in Amsterdam much to the disappointment of the students, who really quite fancied exploring the Dutch capital's "cultural delights". America remain Olympic rugby champions to this day. Freaky, eh?

Not quite "Invincible"

Kiwis denied Grand Slam by scaredy cat Scots

Any team worth its salt has a nickname and you don't get many better monikers than the All Black "Invincibles" that came, saw and most definitely conquered on their 1925 tour of the Home Nations.

The New Zealanders swept all before them throughout their 30-match programme, but were controversially denied a historic Grand Slam when Scotland refused to play them.

The Scots claimed the All Blacks were professional in all but name and decided to sulk. The English claimed Scotland were just being wimps, while the Irish and Welsh thought they'd keep out of it all and go for a nice quiet pint.

The upshot was the New Zealanders, through no fault of their own, weren't quite as "Invincible" as their nickname suggested and Scotland were teased for weeks in the playground for bringing a sick note to school.

Brownlie browned off

All Black becomes first man to get marching orders

New Zealand's Cyril Brownlie went down in rugby history in 1925 when he became the first player ever to be sent off in an international match. Not exactly something to boast about to the grandchildren. Brownlie received his marching orders after what at the time was politely referred to as a "skirmish" with one of the England forwards during the game at Twickenham. Welsh referee Albert Freethy sent him packing and Brownlie and his favourite rubber duck were first into the bath.

Luckily for Cyril, his younger brother Maurice was also playing for the All Blacks that day and he scored a second-half try to wrap up a 17–11 win for the visitors and restore family pride.

Radio waves

Game goes high-tech with live wireless commentary

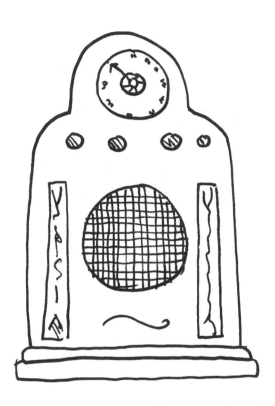

As rugby became more popular, it was only a matter of time before the game reached a wider, mass audience. In 1926, it reached this mega mass when the first-ever radio commentary of a match was broadcast.

The game was Christchurch versus High School Old Boys in New Zealand and, with the commentators faithfully describing assorted acts of skullduggery, violence and mischief, rugger had finally entered the communication age.

Fragrant French forced out

France expelled from the 1931 Five Nations championship amid allegations of illegal player payments and dubious personal hygiene

By 1931, the Home Nations were convinced their scheming Gallic cousins were routinely slipping francs (remember them?) into their players' back pockets. And since the French hadn't even had the decency to try and bribe them with a few nice bottles of claret, they decided to kick them out of the Five Nations competition. The question of the French players' odorous tendencies was already well documented.

Eventually, however, England, Ireland, Scotland and Wales admitted the tournament wasn't quite the same without the flair and fragrance of the French after all (and they were missing the annual weekends away from the wife in Paris) and invited them back to the party after the end of the Second World War.

They'd also belatedly realised it was a bit silly having a Five Nations championship with only four teams.

36 Bledisloe battle begins
Kiwis and Wallabies get it on

In 1931, the Australian and New
Zealand rugby boards admitted
they were both getting bored of
roughing up the Home Nations
and came up with the obvious idea
of pummelling each other to within
an inch of their own lives instead.
The result – The Bledisloe Cup
(donated by New Zealand's
conveniently named Governor-
General Lord Bledisloe) – quickly
became a regular fixture on the
Antipodean sporting calendar and
proved a welcome distraction from
the tiresome task of beating up on
their Northern hemisphere rivals.

Commies join the Union

Rugby breaks through the Iron Curtain in 1933

Communism and the Soviet Union can't have been all bad. Okay, so they were responsible for the Iron Curtain across Europe, the Cold War, ill-fitting jeans and Skoda cars, but there were some positives.

For a start, the Soviet Union embraced rugby in the twentieth century with real enthusiasm and the first game to be played in the USSR was a 1933 clash between

Moscow Dynamo and Moscow PE College played in, yes, you've guessed it, Moscow!

The sport flourished in the decades that followed, although it was thought the secret police would give suspected dissidents the choice of a little one-way trip to Siberia or 80 minutes in the front row when caught. Most plumped for Siberia.

1936 was what you could call a turbulent year in the life of Edward Windsor (*aka* Edward Albert Christian George Andrew Patrick David Windsor). His father, King George V died, he then became King Edward VIII and, by December, he'd sensationally abdicated to marry some American harlot called Wallis Simpson. But the highlight of the year for the short-term monarch must surely have been becoming the patron of the Rugby Football Union.

Whether Edward was actually a rugby fan or was just in it for the free Twickenham tickets to tout to his mates is unclear.

Rugby on the box

The sport joins the televisual age (or whatever they called it back then...)

1938 was a momentous year for rugby as the BBC broadcast live pictures of England's clash with Scotland at Twickenham. Admittedly, there were only about 17 television sets in the whole of the British Isles at the time (and six of those were in for repair) but the coverage was the start of a new era for the game as people watching at home gawped in horror at the antics of the front-row forwards and the incompetence of the referee.

Ban for Alban

Claim costs Davies dear

EXPENSES

Cheeky Welsh student Alban Davies was banned for life from the game in 1938 – for submitting an outrageous claim for £3 in expenses. Being a student, Davies obviously only wanted the money to buy Pot Noodles and Rizlas but the Welsh RFU failed to see the funny side of it (perhaps they needed some Rizlas of their own) and insisted it would break their strict amateur status if they paid up.

Plucky to the last, Davies argued the £3 was the equivalent of his lost earnings when he turned out for the Major Stanley's XV, but since he was an unemployed (and, no doubt, bone idle) student, his argument was about as convincing as Bill Clinton's definition of "sexual relations".

Davies sued the Welsh RFU, lost his case and promptly headed off to the student union to drown his sorrows.

HALF-TIME

Wallabies' wasted trip
Shortest tour on record after outbreak of war

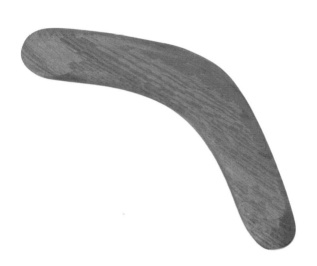

The Australian team selected to visit Britain in 1939 must rate as one of the unluckiest touring teams in the history of the game. It was still in the days when touring sides took boats rather than flew to reach their destination and the hapless Wallabies endured months at sea (thankfully avoiding scurvy and attacks by pirates) to get to Blighty and start their tour.

Almost as soon as their boat docked, however, World War Two broke out across Europe and the Aussies were forced to do a rather morale-sapping, boomeranging, U-turn and return home without playing a single match!

42 Kiwis can fly!

Ground-breaking All Blacks take the aerial route

New Zealanders have always been pioneers of the game and they lived up to that reputation in 1947 when they became the first team to take to the skies. Before 1947, any team touring abroad travelled by sea (see moment 41) so the All Blacks broke new ground when they chartered a flying boat to take them across the Tasman Sea to Australia. David Attenborough nearly choked on his cornflakes because it was the first recorded instance of kiwis actually flying...

Despite the overloaded plane nearly sinking on landing under the weight of the New Zealand players, the idea proved to be an inspired one as the tourists convincingly won the two-Test series against the Wallabies.

McWhirter the winger

Founder of Guinness Book of Records makes Saracens debut

The late, great Norris McWhirter is best remembered as the co-founder of the Guinness Book of Records and for giving the late, also great Roy Castle a plausible excuse to tap dance and play the trumpet every week on children's television.

But before he found fame as the man who could tell you off the top of his head the size of the biggest turnip ever, McWhirter was a talented rugby player who turned out for Saracens in 1947. A former sprinter for Scotland and Great Britain, McWhirter unsurprisingly played on the wing for the London but had to hang up his boots as his trivia career took off.

Aussies get organised at last
ARU is belatedly formed

The first game of rugby Down Under took place in 1864 at Sydney University Club but, despite the instant popularity of the game, it was not until 1949 that the Australian Rugby Union was officially formed, a delay of 85 years.

Exactly why the Aussies moved at such a snail's pace to set up a governing body for the sport is a mystery. Maybe they just didn't give a XXXX.

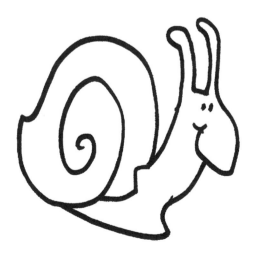

The generation game

Father and son go head-to-head in New Zealand

The 1950 clash between Poverty Bay and Olympians in New Zealand was a strange affair for all concerned because both sides had players called George Nepia in their line-ups.

It was even more confusing because the two Nepias on show were actually father and son – former All Black George Senior in Poverty Bay colours and George Junior turning out for the Olympians.

Mrs Nepia couldn't bear to watch.

46 Packing them in

Record crowd squeeze into Ellis Park and watch Lions roar

The British Lions have always been big box office, but the 1955 squad that travelled to South Africa were arguably the most popular of all.

The tourists had not played the Springboks for 17 long years and, judging by their reaction to the Lions' arrival, the locals had obviously been counting the days until their return.

The first Test of the four-Test series was held in Johannesburg and somehow a stadium-busting 100,000 rugby enthusiasts managed to cram themselves into Ellis Park to watch the action

Unluckily for the South African supporters, the wait definitely wasn't worth it as the Lions held their nerve for a 23–22 win.

Communists get cold feet

Russians scared off rugger by Welshmen

When Welsh club Llanelli sent a side to the USSR in 1957 for the World Youth Games, they could have little imagined the impact their visit would have behind the Iron Curtain.

Reports from the tour said that the ever-present and shady Communist officials were so shocked by the levels of violence they witnessed when the Scarlets met Romanian side Grivita Rosie that they banned the game for nearly 30 years, obviously recognising the threat 30 overweight alcoholics posed to the world superpower.

48 Muddy hell!
Entire Welsh team "sent off" in Cardiff

In 1957 the entire Wales XV were given their marching orders during a Championship clash with Ireland in Cardiff. But it wasn't a case of unprecedented naughtiness that led to their early departure. Cardiff had been deluged with rain and, by the time the game kicked-off, the Arms Park pitch was a mud bath.

Midway through the second-half the referee realised the players' shirts were so muddy he had no idea what was going on (so what's new...?) and ordered the Welsh to nip off and find some clean shirts.

Legend has it that one quick-thinking Irish player joined the mass exodus, had a quick pint and returned to the fray with no-one any the wiser.

49 A rum show

Tricolores hit the bottle to beat Springboks in 1958

The French love of wine is legendary but our friends from across the Channel are also partial to the odd drop of the hard stuff judging by the curious tale of Lucien Mias.

The forward was the captain of the French team that toured South Africa in 1958 and after a draw in the first Test in Cape Town, Mias was desperate to lead his side to a first-ever win over the Springboks in the second Test in Johannesburg.

The match was tight and at half-time Mias retreated to the dressing room to inspire his troops. But rather than going for a stirring speech, threats of physical violence or handing out a plate of oranges, he opted to down half a bottle of rum and say very little at all.

Amazingly, his unorthodox approach worked as the French clung on for a famous 9–5 win, Mias staggering off the pitch to finish what he'd started and the South African players thanking their lucky stars he hadn't breathed on them.

 Jamaica in

Tropical island joins the club

Rugby's worldwide popularity has grown with the years and it chalked up another global outpost in 1959 when the Jamaican RFU was formed. It should actually have been founded in 1958 but no-one was in any great hurry, man.

Jamaica now boasts over 10,000 adult players, 10 senior clubs and a mysteriously large number of foreign teams wanting to arrange holida..., er, tours of their country.

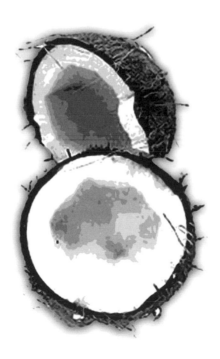

P-p-p-pick up a Penguin

New touring team leave wives behind to promote global goodwill in rugby (and drink a lot)

The famous (or perhaps that should really be infamous) Penguins invitational touring side was set up in 1959 by Sidcup players Tony Mason and Alan Wright, at a stroke creating a whole new generation of rugby widows.

Since the Penguins' formation, they have toured countless countries (well, 57 if you're counting), graced many a 15- and seven-a-side tournament and, of course, drunk innumerable bars dry in the name of rugby.

Established to promote goodwill in the game, the Penguins are, to be fair, also a force to be reckoned with on the pitch, particularly on the sevens circuit, winning consecutive Middlesex Sevens titles at Twickenham in 1999 and 2000. Both victories, of course, were good excuses for a drink-up.

"No, my husband can't come out to play"

52 Literary laughs

First seminal rugby humour book published
(it wasn't as funny as this one... obviously)

In 1960, The Art of Coarse Rugby, a
humorous tome by Michael Green hit the
bookshelves (the shelves didn't retaliate).
In one fell literary swoop, the book
confirmed what everyone had suspected all
along: i.e. rugby was largely a game played
by overweight alcoholics desperate to get
out of the house and into the pub.

It was an instant hit among those in the
rugby fraternity who could actually read and
is still a rich source of humour for all those
club captains desperately looking for some
good jokes for their end-of-season speeches.

But the book was not as popular with
referees – probably because they were the
butt of most of the gags. For example: "The
first half is invariably much longer than
the second. This is partly because of
the late kick-off, but is also caused
by the unfitness of the referee."

53 Crauste coshed
Frenchman attacked by irate Kiwi fan

Everyone knows rugby can be a violent game – and let's face it, for most that's the appeal – but it isn't always a size 12 boot to the head or a sly punch in a ruck that players should be wary of. France's ill-tempered tour (when are French tours anything else?) of New Zealand in 1961 was a classic example.

The French were embroiled in countless brawls on the trip (mostly on the field) and their match against South Canterbury was no different. Late in the second-half, the home side's Eddie Smith was pole-axed by a stiff-arm tackle. Just to rub salt into the wound, French skipper Michel Crauste decided to pick the prostrate Kiwi up off the ground ... and then throw him back down again.

A female New Zealand supporter rushed out to remonstrate with the dastardly Monsieur Crauste and the crowd nearly died laughing when she landed a punch on the back of his head. The irate intruder was led away, the game carried on and Crauste never lived down the shame of publicly being beaten up by a woman.

Willie John makes "99" call

Lions' legend McBride has the Springboks' number

The legendary Willie John McBride was a colossus of the game. After making his international debut against England in 1962, he went on to win 63 caps for Ireland (there was a national hat shortage, apparently...) and captained the all-conquering 1974 Lions tour to South Africa.

During the tour, the no-nonsense Irishman realised his team needed to combat the Springboks' notoriously physical approach (a polite way of saying

they were a bunch of thugs) and came up with the now legendary "99" call. On hearing the call from their skipper, all the Lions were expected to wade into whatever fracas was going on and introduce the naughty South African players to Mr Fist.

The tactic was a huge success, the Springboks mended their mischievous ways (after a few black eyes and stitches) and the Lions won a series in South Africa at the seventh time of asking.

"That's not what I meant by '99'"

Plague alert

Smallpox causes postponement and rescheduled game proves to be poxy

Originally scheduled for March, the 1962 Five Nations game between Ireland and Wales had to be rearranged twice because of an outbreak of smallpox in South Wales. Perhaps wisely, the health authorities decided it would probably be a bad idea to have thousands of drunken, pox-ridden Welshmen roaming the streets of the Irish capital, passing the plague on to their Celtic cousins.

The match finally went ahead in November the following year once all the itching and unsightly sores had cleared up but it proved to be a bit of an anticlimax as the game ended in a thoroughly uninspiring 3–3 stalemate.

Cocky Campo

Outspoken Wallaby winger is born Down Under

1962 was a not a great year in history. Marilyn Monroe died, the Cuban Missile Crisis reached its bum-tightening climax and *Hancock's Half Hour* disappeared from our screens.

Even worse was to come, however, because it was also the year that Mr and Mrs Campese gave birth (well, only Mrs Campese to be fair) to little David Campese in the Australian Capital Territory. "Whingeing Poms" were reported to be his first words.

The follicly challenged winger went on to play 101 times for the Wallabies, won the 1991 World Cup but appeared to spend most of his career slagging off the English.

One of the most gifted and well-balanced players of his generation (he had chips on both shoulders), his finest moment came in 2003, in the wake of England's World Cup triumph, when he was forced to parade down Oxford Street in London wearing a sandwich board reading "I admit the best team won".

He is currently pacing up and down Oxford Street wearing a sandwich board reading "Discount golf sale". Hopefully.

57 Bore draw
Scotland and New Zealand fire blanks

The last recorded instance of a 0–0 scoreline at international level was in 1964 when Scotland faced New Zealand at Murrayfield and both sides failed to conjure up a single score between them. Which frankly takes some doing in 80 minutes. Unless you're blind. And very, very unlucky.

The paying fans may have felt pretty cheesed off after the bore draw but the Scottish players were delighted – they got in for free and it was also the closest they had ever come to beating the mighty All Blacks.

Scotland still haven't managed to overcome New Zealand to this day – making their 1964 dullathon a bizarre highlight in their history.

58 Injury update Pt. 1
Rule makers give green light to substitutes

Pre-1968 rugby players were unquestionably a hardy bunch. In the days before padding and proper training, players took a fearful beating on a regular basis. And when they managed to escape the angry clutches of their neglected wives, things were even worse out on the pitch.

It was also the era when replacements for injuries (genuine or fake) were banned, meaning players were often forced to soldier on despite having limbs hanging off or half of the opposition front row's studs embedded in their skull.

That all changed in 1968, however, when the International Board finally bowed to pressure from overworked physios and maimed players everywhere and agreed to allow injury substitutions. Which was nice of them.

Injury update Pt. 2

French star comes a cropper before kick-off

To get injured during a match is bad luck. To get injured even before the first whistle is just plain carelessness. One of the most ridiculous examples of a player failing to stay in one piece before the first whistle occurred in 1969 when Scotland travelled to Paris to play France.

The French were confident of victory in the changing room as kick-off approached and, when the call came to take the pitch, they charged out with chests puffed out and hearts racing. Sadly, however, winger Jean-Pierre Salut was obviously a little too pumped up and forgot one or two basics – like watching where the hell he was going.

All his team-mates successfully managed to negotiate the stairs between the changing room and the pitch but poor old Salut came an absolute cropper and broke his ankle.

One of the substitutes was hastily pressed into action, Scotland pulled off a surprise victory and Salut's blushes were made profitable by the 250 francs he earned after sending the tape of the incident to the French equivalent of *You've Been Framed*.

The Irish make good comedians, the English make good subject material. Or so the saying goes. But the theory was severely put to the test in 1972 when the two countries met in the Five Nations in Dublin.

For once Ireland were happy to see the English – both Scotland and Wales had refused to play that year because of the Troubles.

England made the trip and obligingly lost 16–12 to the men in green. At the post-match dinner, England captain John Pullin stood up to deliver his speech and had everyone in stitches with his opening line, "We may not be much good but at least we turn up."

Murdoch goes missing

Disgraced All Black goes AWOL after hotel punch-up

Andy Warhol once predicted we'd all have our 15 minutes of fame, but in New Zealander Keith Murdoch's case it was 30 years of infamy after being sent home from the All Blacks' 1972 tour of Wales.

The Kiwis had just narrowly beaten the Welsh in Cardiff, with Murdoch scoring the winning try, but the post-match celebrations didn't exactly go according to plan when Murdoch got into a public fight with a hotel guard. The press had a field day and Murdoch was put on the first plane home in disgrace. The thing is, Murdoch was so ashamed that rather than return to New Zealand and face the music (well, would you want to listen to Crowded House?) he jumped off the flight in Australia (no, it wasn't in the air at the time) and promptly disappeared into the Australian Outback.

Nothing was heard from the black sheep for the next 30 years until the Australian police made his whereabouts public because they were looking for him as a witness in a murder case.

It's a massive tie!

Dead heat in closest Five Nations in history

The start of every Five Nations competition is always tinged with excitement and hope for every fan desperate for something to celebrate come the end of the season. In 1973, however, every beer-loving supporter had an excuse to raise their glasses (as if they needed one) after the tournament finished in an amazing five-way tie.

It was in the days before the title was decided on points difference and, with all five teams winning two and losing two of their four fixtures, the title had to be shared.

Mercifully, it was also in the days before a trophy was awarded to the winners, and an unseemly and no doubt violent debate about sharing the (non-existent) silverware was thus avoided.

Rugby of the Gods
Greatest-ever try scored in Cardiff

It was a religious man who introduced the Welsh to rugby (see No. 3), so it was fitting that arguably the most heavenly moment witnessed in the history of the game should take place in Cardiff.

The match, of course, was the Barbarians' clash with the All Blacks at Cardiff Arms Park and the moment, Gareth "The Saint" Edwards' legendary try *aka* "The Try".

A beautiful, dramatic score that had millions on the edge of their seats, The Try went, in the words of commentator Cliff Morgan, something like this...

"Kirpatrick to Williams. This is great stuff. Phil Bennett covering, chased by Alistair Scown. Brilliant, oh, that's brilliant. John Williams. Pullin. John Dawes, great dummy. To David, Tom David, the halfway line. Brilliant by Quinnell. This Gareth Edwards. A dramatic start. WHAT A SCORE!"

Kenneth Wolstenholme, eat your heart out...

Bomber belts Wheel

First dismissals in Championship history

The 1973 Five Nations clash between Wales and Ireland in Cardiff went down in the rugby record books for all the wrong reasons when Ireland's Willie "The Blackrock Bomber" Duggan and Wales' Geoff "Sorry, I haven't got a nickname" Wheel became the first players ever to be sent off in a championship match.

The pugilistic pair got their marching orders after punching each other senseless right under the ref's nose who, try as he might not to notice the incident, had no option but to send the feisty duo for an early bath. Whether they bathed separately or not remains unclear.

65 Party déjà vu

Irish celebrate second centenary in five years!

The Irish will find any excuse for a party (okay, so they don't even need a reason) but they came up with an absolute corker in the '70s to justify a bizarre double celebration.

The Irish Rugby Union was first formed in 1874 and the centenary celebrations were duly observed with a Guinness or 10 in 1974 to mark the occasion.

But then some (possibly alcoholic) clever clogs pointed out that Ulster had not been present at the original 1874 meeting and, in fact, the Irish Union was reformed in 1879 when Ulster finally got their act together and bothered to show up. Cue a second centenary celebration in 1979 and oodles more Guinness. Which is pretty much like every other day in Ireland anyway. Hurrah!

Anderson causes Argy-bargy
Irishman sparks diplomatic row

High jinks are a staple of any rugby tour along with the removal of wedding rings, countless alcohol-related forfeits and sleepless nights for nervous hotel managers. In 1980, however, Irishman Willie Anderson managed to up the ante when he got himself arrested on a friendly tour of Argentina and sparked a huge diplomatic row.

After a predictably liquid night out, Anderson was roaming the streets when he spotted through bleary eyes an Argentinian flag fluttering in the breeze. Eager to return home with a souvenir (other than kidney failure), Anderson shinned up the pole and nicked the flag. Unfortunately, when he came back down to earth, he was nicked by the local constabulary and carted off to the clink. No doubt, Anderson thought he'd be left alone to sober up and then sent on his way, but the Argentinians had other ideas and the unlucky Irishman spent days in jail as the country's military junta enjoyed the chance to flex their muscles.

Anderson was eventually released and he went on to star for Ireland. Argentina went on to invade the Falklands.

Not so smart...

Proof positive you should really stick to beer

Rugby players have always been known to partake of the odd drink or two after a game, but in the stomach-churning case of England forward Colin Smart it was a drink too far in the early 1980s.

Smart was part of the England team that played France in Paris and after the game joined his team-mates for the usual post-match dinner, speeches and random displays of male nudity. Unfortunately, Smart turned up late and by the time he arrived he had no idea that the rest of the England players had filled their souvenir bottles of aftershave – a present from their fragrant French hosts – with water. All except one particular bottle.

It wasn't long before the England players dared each other to drink the "aftershave" and Smart, seeing the others emptying their doctored bottles, followed suit and downed the perfume. Luckily for him he didn't have time to worry why everyone was laughing at him as French paramedics whisked him off in an ambulance to have his stomach pumped. And they say forwards aren't blessed with brains...

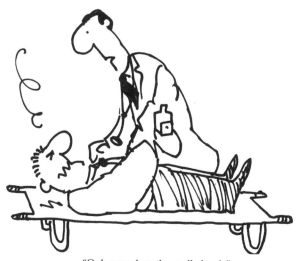

"Ooh, your breath smells lovely"

Secretive Springboks

Record low crowd as South Africa dodge protests

When is a crowd not, in fact, a crowd? Probably when there's only 35 people in it, which was the case when South Africa played America in New York in 1981.

The reason for the staggeringly poor attendance – a record low for an international match – was the apartheid regime and the touring Springboks' fears that the match, like their previous tour games, would be disrupted by anti-apartheid protests.

So in true cloak-and-dagger style the two sides decided to switch both the day and the venue for the fixture to throw the protesters off the scent. It worked rather too well though because the genuine fans had no idea what was going on either and the 35 people who did turn up in Glenville for the game thought it was some sort of car boot sale.

For the record, South Africa won the game 38–7 and then got the hell out of there as fast as they could.

"I'm just going to get a drink. Hold my seat for me..."

Erica streak wows the nation

Twickenham gets its first ever streaker

Think nudity and rugby and distressing images of hairy-arsed, sweaty men drinking to excess spring to mind like a post-traumatic stress flashback.

But that all changed during half-time of a game between England and Australia at Twickenham in January 1982 when a buxom bookshop assistant from Petersfield called Erica Roe whipped off her top, unleashed her 40-inch chest and ran out onto the hallowed turf of HQ.

Miss Roe's curvy chest was an instant and national hit and her antics inspired a new generation of female (and,

sadly, male) streakers, who would become a familiar sight at rugby and other sporting venues in the years to come.

"All I know is that I had my hands behind my back and I unhitched my bra. And the rest is history," Erica later confessed. "I can't give a straight answer as to why it happened except that I'd had a few beers and was a bit eccentric. It must have lasted 40 seconds, but I've become famous for my boobs."

Indeed.

Tragically, Roe moved to Portugal not long after her little show – depriving the nation of one its greatest natural, um, assets.

Perhaps it was fate that, in the same year as Erica Roe made such a big impact at Twickenham, women's rugby would see its first-ever international match staged.

The game was between France and the Netherlands in Paris but it was far from what you could call a thriller, with the French scraping home by a 4–0 scoreline.

The biggest drama of the day didn't come until after the match when press photographers were told that, no, they wouldn't be able to take any shots of the team bath.

They took one hell of a beating

Rebel French side succumb to super-sized defeats

French third division club Vergt gave a whole new meaning to the term "one-sided match" in 1984 when a fit of pique saw the club lose by record scores on successive weekends.

Vergt were furious at the suspension of four of their key players for various acts of skullduggery but, rather than take it on the chin, they decided to sulk and enforce a industrial dispute-style "go-slow" in protest.

So when they came up against Gujah-Misters in a league clash they were not exactly at their most motivated and were beaten by a mind-boggling 236–0 scoreline.

But if you think that's bad, think again. The following week they played Lavardac and, still in protest mode, they went down by a staggering 350–0, a record mauling in anyone's book.

Peace-loving ref

Ref George Crawford gets so fed up with the fighting during an Anglo-Welsh clash between Bristol and Newport in 1985 that he walks off the pitch

"Hey man, what's with all this fighting? Where's the love? Why don't we all just take a chill pill? Groovy. Violence never solved anything after all. How about we talk about it over a cup of dandelion tea and a nettle muffin, yeah? Cool, man, cool. Like the great man said, make love not war. Give peace a chance. Right, sod you lot, I'm off..."

So said our George before leaving the field. Probably.

New balls please...
Shelford shrugs off eye-watering injury

Rugby's a game for hard men and they have rarely come any harder than New Zealand's Wayne "Buck" Shelford. If, however, you are of a squeamish disposition then it's probably not a good idea to read the rest of this page. Don't say you weren't warned.

Shelford was in action for the All Blacks against France in Nantes in 1986 when he was caught by a misplaced French stud – they'd been aiming for his head but settled for his groin. Now "Buck" knew something wasn't quite right down under (and he wasn't thinking about the acting in *Neighbours*) and, on inspection of his crown jewels, he realised the stud had ripped his scrotum. Even worse, one of his testicles was dangling out of the wound like some sort of macabre conker.

Amazingly, he didn't faint on the spot and actually told the stunned physio that he wanted him to pop it back in, sew up his scrotum and, if at all possible, stop being sick all over the place.

The deed was done, Shelford carried on playing but, to rub salt into the wound (thankfully, not literally), the French held on for a 16–3 victory. Ouch.

Rugger goes a bit global

All Blacks win inaugural World Cup competition on home soil

The first rugby World Cup was jointly staged by Australia and New Zealand in 1987, the first time the rugby-playing fraternity had ever got together en masse, shared a few beers and squeezed in a few games for good measure.

The northern hemisphere sides had initially been a bit sniffy about the whole thing but Australia and New Zealand sweet-talked them into it and the competition finally got the go ahead.

The tournament did not disappoint – unless you happened to be from England, Scotland or Ireland as all three teams failed to make it past the quarter-finals. Wales made the semis but got stuffed by the All Blacks.

The final was held in Auckland between the New Zealanders and France. In a pattern that wouldn't be broken until England's 2003 triumph, the southern hemisphere side got the better of the one from the north, the All Blacks running out 29–9 winners.

Will marry for tickets!

New Zealand rugby fans would do anything to watch their heroes in the 1987 World Cup final, as this cheeky personal ad proved...

- **CERTIFIED GENIUS** seeks stupid girl to bring out my inner idiot. Voicebox 101010
- **SHY GUY** seeks famous film star to share their wealth and celebrity with me. Just don't expect me to talk to your friends (especially if you know Michael Winner). Voicebox 287666
- **MAN CALLED DEREK** seeks woman called Marion with long brown hair, a 32CC chest who used to live with me in Leamington Spa. I haven't seen you since you said you were going down the shops to buy turkey twizzlers. Voicebox 111999
- **BUILDER LOOKING FOR LOVE** Let me throw you in the concrete mixer of my love and turn you into a nice garden ornament for my patio. Voicebox 732901
- **HOLY AND OLD** ...

- **I'M ELECTRIC!** I'm from a family full of eccentrics. I like talking about plugs. I will short circuit your brain. 100% guarantee. Voicebox 620186
- **FREAKISHLY TALL** professional limbo dancer. Very bendy. Seeks woman with head in the clouds. Voicebox 356271
- **YOUNG RUGBY SUPPORTER** of good appearance and sound health offers hand in marriage to any young lady with two tickets for the World Cup final. Please send photograph of the tickets. Voicebox 001995
- **WILL CARLING IMPERSONATOR** I dress like Will Carling, I eat the same food as Will Carling and I hit myself repeatedly in the face to look exactly like him. If you like Will Carling, you'll love me. Voicebox 288890

76 Trophy tomfoolery
Calcutta Cup gets a good kicking

Post-match dinners are notoriously boozy affairs during which hatchets are buried, friendships forged and waitresses' bottoms pinched. The 1988 shindig in Edinburgh after England's narrow win over Scotland was no different. Scotland's John Jeffrey and England's Dean Richards were particularly "lubricated" and, in one of those moments that seem to make perfect sense only when you're drunk, the pair decided to take the Calcutta Cup – the historic trophy awarded to the winners of Anglo-Scottish clashes – on a tour of Edinburgh.

It wasn't long before they were playing football with the priceless silverware in the streets of the Scottish capital and in the process caused thousands of pounds worth of damage to the trophy. Not so much a case of "my cup runneth over" as "my cup gets runneth over".

Richards received a surprisingly lenient one-match ban from the RFU while his partner in crime was slapped with a six-month suspension by the furious Scottish RFU.

77 Sweet chariot
England team gets its own anthem

No-one is quite sure why (or when) England fans adopted the nineteenth-century African-American spiritual song *Swing Low, Sweet Chariot* as the team's unofficial anthem. Some believed the lack of long, complicated words was the deciding factor while others argued "carry me home" had a certain resonance with the average supporter.

But whatever the reason, the tune is now synonymous with the England team much in the same way that "Who's the self-abuser in the black?" always conjures up images of incompetent referees.

The first time anyone can remember the song being sung at Twickenham (not many people can remember much after a day out at Twickers) was in 1988 when England played Ireland. It worked a treat too as England ran out convincing 35–3 winners.

Longlife Leonard
Big Jase makes England debut in Argentina in 1990

The most-capped player in the history of the international game is Jason Leonard, the Harlequins, England and Lions prop, whose barrel-chest and ever-present stubble were a fixture in a record-breaking 114 Test matches during the 1990s and whatever we're supposed to call the decade after that.

A carpenter by trade, Leonard made his England debut in 1990 in Argentina and he remained a first choice for his country for nearly 15 years before succumbing to the lure of beer and pies and retiring in 2004.

But big Jase wasn't a prolific try-scorer in his 114 Tests and, just like this story, only crossed the line...

... once (against Argentina at Twickenham in 1996).

Murrayfield mayhem
England denied Grand Slam by delirious Scots

By 1990, England hadn't won the Grand Slam for a decade but were the overwhelming favourites to clinch the clean sweep against Scotland in Edinburgh. The unbeaten Scots had done it six years earlier but still no-one gave them a prayer of repeating the trick at Murrayfield. The stage was set for one of the great sporting upsets.

Sure enough, the Scots tore into the visitors like turbo-charged William Wallaces and England began to wilt like a limp lettuce in a heatwave.

The defining moment came in the second-half when Scottish winger Tony Stanger got the luck of the bounce after Gavin Hastings had chipped ahead, grabbed the loose ball and went over for the only try of the match.

The roar could be heard in London, Scotland held on for their most famous win over the old enemy and the party to end all parties began.

80 Is God a rugby fan?

Game abandoned after divine intervention

The Church's view on rugby remains unclear. Sunday fixtures can't go down well for a start and it would be naive to think some of the traditional post-match revelries are going to impress the local vicar. In 1991, however, the "big man upstairs" gave his clearest signal yet he's not a big fan when America's game with France in Colorado was abandoned because of an act of God.

Everything was it should have been until the second-half when a bolt of lightning lit up the sky and then struck the stadium's electronic scoreboard, which blew up rather impressively. The game was called off and many of the players promised never to blaspheme again.

EXTRA TIME!

Rugger goes really global
The (square) eyes have it

Rugby really puts itself on the map with the second World Cup in 1991, hosted by the English. In England!

While the first tournament Down Under four years earlier had been a charmingly low-key affair that people viewed as a bit of a novelty, this time around the organisers went to town, had a superb meal, fine wines and a few nightcaps.

It was obviously worth the effort as an estimated 1.6 billion people worldwide bunked off work, disconnected the phone, settled into their armchairs and watched the action. Which is one hell of a lot of pizzas, cans of beer and trial separations.

For the record, Australia beat/lucked out against (delete as applicable) England in the final at Twickenham.

Yanks win women's World Cup

Women's game goes global ... in Wales!

The first women's World Cup was staged in The Principality in 1991 and the fairer sex finally got the stage they deserved to display their undeniable talent. Rugby talent, that is.

The players courageously overcame the lack of hair-drier sockets in the changing rooms and the tournament was an unqualified success (well, New Zealand didn't win it for a start...). With 12 teams competing, it proved the women's game was growing in popularity worldwide.

The final was between England and the USA team, with the Americans emerging 19–6 winners.

Sevens heaven

England upset the odds (and the Aussies) to be crowned world champions

Even though Ned Haig (see No. 10) had cunningly invented sevens rugby over a hundred years earlier, the game had always been seen as an amusing but slightly silly diversion, much like a round of crazy golf or the Eurovision Song Contest.

That all changed in 1993, however, when Scotland staged the Sevens World Cup and England, believe it or not, actually beat the Australians at something. No, really.

No-one gave England a prayer going into the tournament but, with future stars like Lawrence Dallaglio and Tim Rodber in storming form and speed merchant Andy Harriman doing a great impression of the Road Runner, they battled their way through to the final and a clash with the Wallabies at Murrayfield.

Pre-match, the nation breathed a collective sigh of resignation but England broke with all convention, played a blinder and actually beat the convicts. Which let's face it, doesn't happen every day.

Centurion centre

100-cap Frenchman sets new world record

The first man in rugby history to win a century of international caps was France's Philippe Sella, who reached the milestone in the Tricolores' victory over New Zealand in Christchurch in 1994.

Born in Tonneins in 1962, Sella was a tough and talented centre who just kept on going and going and going after his debut against Romania in 1982.

Rebuffing persistent offers to advertise Duracell batteries, the French star finally realised enough was enough after the 1995 World Cup and hung up his boots. The boots were delighted.

In total, Sella won 111 caps, scored 30 tries and played in three World Cups. He signed for Saracens in 1996 to top up his pension fund, played for a couple of seasons to show willing and then headed back off to France to admire his extensive collection of headwear.

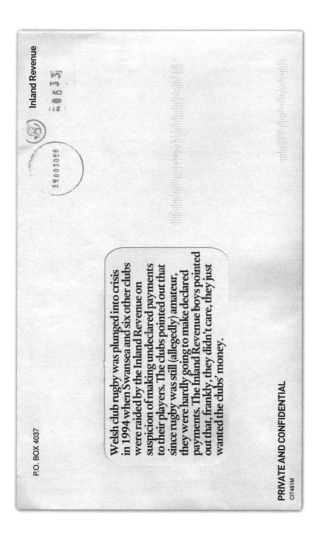

P.O. BOX 4037

Inland Revenue

Welsh club rugby was plunged into crisis in 1994 when Swansea and six other clubs were raided by the Inland Revenue on suspicion of making undeclared payments to their players. The clubs pointed out that since rugby was still (allegedly) amateur, they were hardly going to make declared payments. The Inland Revenue boys pointed out that, frankly, they didn't care, they just wanted the clubs' money.

PRIVATE AND CONFIDENTIAL

CIT481M

Carling's clanger

England captain talks himself out of job ... and then back in again!

When he wasn't preening himself, writing management-speak motivation books and getting rather too close to certain members of the Royal Family, Will Carling also found time to play some rugby. The England captain also found more than enough time to wind up pretty much anyone whom he came across and although it was a blessing to his beleaguered postman at Christmas time (who was sick of all the hate mail), it also meant he could count his friends on one hand.

Carling's most spectacular clanger came in the build-up to the 1995 Rugby World Cup when, in an unguarded moment, he said on camera: "If the game is run properly as a professional game, you do not need 57 old farts running rugby."

The old farts in question were members of the RFU committee and, once they'd been wheeled out of the Twickenham bar, they sacked him for his dashing impertinence.

The twist in the tale was Carling was actually reinstated after an outpouring of public support. Just not from Buckingham Palace, obviously.

"Parp!"

Alright for All Blacks

Kiwis crush Japan at World Cup

The problem with the
record books is you have to keep
rewriting them, which is why it's always
advisable to use a pencil and have a rubber handy,
especially when the mighty All Blacks are in action.
This was certainly the case at the 1995 World Cup in
South Africa when New Zealand played Japan in a group match
in Bloemfontein. Of course, everyone expected the Kiwis to win
at a canter (or maybe a gallop) but not even the most ardent All
Black fan (or pessimistic Japanese supporter for that matter) could
have predicted the carnage that was to follow.
To call the contest "one-sided" would be akin to describing the
Titanic as slightly unseaworthy and from the first whistle
the hapless Japanese were put to the (samurai) sword.
Eighty minutes later and New Zealand had racked
up a record 145–17 victory, scoring 21 tries.
The land of the rising sun had been
well and truly eclipsed.

Jonah the giant

Lomu crushes Carling's England ... and makes millions in the process

"There's no doubt about it, he's a big bastard." The immortal words of Scotland captain Gavin Hastings, talking about the Kiwi winger and human bulldozer *aka* Jonah "The Giant" Lomu.

A truly terrifying 19 stone of prime New Zealand beef on the hoof, Lomu became rugby's first true global superstar at the 1995 World Cup in South Africa when he and his size 13s quite literally trampled all over England and their dreams of reaching the final.

He was a mere 20 years old when the two sides met in Durban but his wholly accurate impression of a runaway train in a hurry soon did for England as the young All Black ran over or through what seemed like every single player in a white shirt in a devastating four-try burst.

Even though New Zealand lost to hosts South Africa in the final, the world was at Lomu's humungous feet and, careful not to squash it, he was soon earning big bucks promoting computer games, sports equipment and anything else the advertisers could think of.

A big bastard with an even bigger bastard bank account...

NEWBANK & CO

07-01-16
12343678

Date *Rugby's Lucky Day* **1995**

Pay **NZ, AUSTRALIA & S.AFRICA**
Three hundred and forty million
pounds only

£ **340,000,000**

UNCLE RUPERT

Uncle Rupert

"301021" 07"00111-9 12667892"

Top-flight rugby finally waved goodbye to its amateur days in 1995 when New Zealand, Australia and South Africa had a cosy chat with media mogul Rupert Murdoch, took in a show and then decided it was time to start lining their (oh, and the players') pockets.

The move came in the wake of the World Cup. The game was becoming more and more popular and Murdoch was keen to broadcast as much top-quality egg-chasing action as possible on his News Corporation network, offering a mouth-watering £340 million to screen the newly created Tri-Nations and Super-12 competitions.

New Zealand, Australia and South Africa tried to keep a straight face, failed miserably and bit Murdoch's hand off without a second thought. The northern hemisphere countries pretended to be appalled at the move while secretly working out how much they could earn and then went along with the whole thing.

Like a prop forward who's taken one too many knocks on the head, things have never been quite the same since...

Devereux detained
Legal landmark after broken jaw and court case

The cynics say rugby is no more than legalised violence (and what exactly is wrong with that?) but that doesn't mean absolutely anything goes as Simon Devereux discovered to his cost in 1995.

The Welsh international was playing in a club match for Gloucester against Rosslyn Park when he broke the jaw of Park player Jamie Cowie.

But rather than the time-honoured pint and a handshake in the bar afterwards, Devereux was charged with GBH (not in the bar), convicted (in court, obviously) and hauled off to chokey (in a van) for a nine-month stretch. All of which put a bit of a dampener on Devereux's season.

Wainwright to the rescue
Scotland star saves fan's life

"Is there a doctor in the house?" became "Is there a doctor on the pitch?" in 1995 when Scotland flanker Rob Wainwright swapped his studs for stethoscope to save a fan's life.

Wainwright was playing in a league clash for West Hartlepool against Wasps when an SOS went out for a medic to attend to a supporter who had just suffered a heart attack. Not a single doctor (or married one for that matter) could be found in the crowd and things were looking bleak for the palpitating fan, who by now had lost consciousness.

Cue Wainwright, a qualified army medic, who abandoned the game, grabbed his white coat and did whatever clever doctors do in such circumstances. The upshot was the man thankfully lived, Wainwright was hailed a hero and, in future, rugby tickets were issued with a health warning.

England expelled

Satellite deal sparks unholy Five Nations row

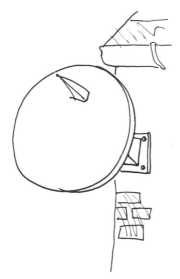

England have not always enjoyed the most cordial of relations with their Five (now Six) Nations rivals but they hit an all-time low in 1996 when the country that invented the game was thrown out of the historic competition.

England's crime was to negotiate a separate TV rights deal with a certain well-known satellite company, leaving the other four countries frankly a bit strapped for cash and just a tad miffed. In retaliation, the furious four got together and decided to show England who was boss, kicking them out of the tournament until they'd come to their senses and agreed a collective deal.

Reasoning they might have a problem keeping their new satellite friends happy when they now had no fixtures to actually play, the RFU hung its head in shame, ripped up the deal and went off to say sorry through gritted teeth to France, Scotland, Ireland and Wales.

England were duly readmitted, the competition went ahead as planned and everyone promised not to mention it again.

No more Oscars

Final curtain for feigners and fakers as subs get the green li

Oscar-winning injury simulations
became a thing of the past in 1996
when the International Rugby
Board announced teams could
make three tactical substitutions
during a game whether the
replaced player was hurt or not.
The new directive finally ended
the dubious days of players
limping off with a badly sprained
fingernail or dislocated ego.

"I've really scratched the nail this time"

(106)

Car trouble

Hapless Halpin halts Cup tie

Many matches have been held up for bizarre reasons (streakers, stray dogs, UFO landings) but they don't come much more strange than the unscheduled break in London Irish and Leicester's Pilkington Cup semi-final in 1996.

Midway through the second-half, the PA announcer read out a car registration number and asked the owner to urgently remove it because it was blocking access to the car park. The crowd went silent as they waited for the miscreant motorist to take the walk of shame and shift their car. Not a soul moved until the penny dropped and red-faced London Irish prop Gary Halpin had to dash off the field to find his keys in the changing room, leaving the 29 other bemused players twiddling their thumbs out on the pitch.

Halpin finally located his keys, threw them to a friend to get the job done and quickly rejoined the fray. The crowd loved it, the Exiles lost the game and Halpin never lived it down.

Samoan-turned-All Black Va'aiga Tuigamala (try saying that after a few aperitifs) became rugby's first £1 million player in 1997 when Newcastle splashed the cash to lure him away from rugby league side Wigan.

Inga the Winger, as he was known, was built like the proverbial stone outhouse but surprisingly quick with it and in many ways was a prototype of the younger Jonah Lomu. Only shorter and with more tattoos. And, believe it or not, even scarier-looking.

Born in Faleasiu in Western Samoa, Tuigamala was a fearsome sight on the pitch but a God-fearing man off it, who could often be found deep in prayer when not playing. His opponents tended to save their praying for match day.

Shouldering on

Players pad up ... but it's not cricket

Rugby's hard-earned hard-man image took a terrible blow in 1997 when shoulder pads were legalized. Suddenly players looked more and more like pampered American footballers. Or Lucy Ewing in '80s soap *Dallas*. Or, even worse, rugby league players.

What old William Webb Ellis would have made of it all is debateable, but the floodgates had been well and truly opened and a new generation of players could now protect their precious shoulders without fear of ridicule. The big girls.

Yellow card joy

Sin bins give lazy players licence to chill

The Tri-Nations (shouldn't that be Try-Nations?) witnessed the first use of the yellow card in rugby history in 1997, giving wrathful referees worldwide the option of sending naughty players to the ominously named "Sin bin" for 10 minutes rather than an early (and permanent) bath.

It was designed to give officials more leeway when it came to foul play, but it soon occurred to more wily (and lazy) players that a yellow card was a brilliant way to get a nice 10-minute sit down and maybe even a Pina Colada whenever they fancied it. All without the shame of actually being sent off.

Clive the office(less) boy
New England coach finds room for improvement

Clive Woodward may have gone on to experience World Cup glory during his seven-year reign as England coach but his first day in the job in 1997 did not bode well for the future.

Like a child on his first day back at school, shiny new satchel on his shoulder and freshly sharpened pencils at the ready, Woodward turned up at Twickenham bursting with ideas about how to transform England into World Champions. And probably plans to end world conflict and poverty as well.

Unfortunately, the RFU were not quite as enthusiastic. In fact, they seemed downright apathetic – they hadn't even bothered to sort out an office for him, so Woodward spent his first day at the office without, er, an office.

Instead, the knighted one decided to share the receptionist's desk in the corridor as he began to plot his rugby revolution and was only mildly annoyed when he realised he couldn't take his first training session in the stationery cupboard.

"No, I won't make the bloody tea..."

Dopey Dallaglio stripped

Lozza loses England captain's armband over tabloid exposé

Lawrence Dallaglio was stripped off the England captaincy in 1999 after becoming the victim of a less-than-elaborate *News of the World* sting. The star confessed to an undercover female reporter (and it certainly seemed he wanted to get her under his covers) that he'd both taken and dealt in class A drugs in the past.

The Sunday tabloid couldn't believe their luck, splashed the revelations all over their front page and Dallaglio was relieved of the captaincy.

Dragged in front of the cameras to explain himself, Lozza (looking suitably sheepish) claimed he'd made it all up to impress the rather attractive reporter, clearly reasoning it was better to be seen as a pathetic liar on the pull than some kind of drug fiend.

The England team rallied around (they couldn't score anywhere else), the *News of the World* found another sap to torment and Martin Johnson became the new England captain. Who says drugs don't have beneficial side-effects?

"I never read the tabloids – they make it up…"
"This time, I think he made it all up for them…"

Lightning Leslie
Kilted Kiwi touches down in record time

The fastest try in the history of the Five (or Six) Nations came in 1999 when Scotland took on Wales at Murrayfield.

The Welsh kicked off and Scotland's New Zealand-born centre John Leslie (no, not the cocaine-snorting, sex video-making TV presenter) gathered the high ball and set off for the line (no pun intended).

Maybe the Welsh team had had a late night and one or two too many wee drams because none of the visitors seemed inclined to tackle Leslie, who quite reasonably made the most of his good fortune and galloped over in a sizzling 10.8 seconds after the first whistle.

The Murrayfield crowd went mad, Wales were hopping mad and Leslie was out of breath.

101 Six appeal
Five Nations welcomes newest member

The Five Nations finally became the Six Nations in 2000 when Italy were sent an invite to the annual party and turned up on the dot of eight.

The Italians had been badgering for years to be admitted to the tournament and after countless fact-finding missions to the bars, restaurants and five-star hotels of Rome (not to mention Venice, Florence, Milan and Sardinia) the diligent competition committee folk finally relented and opened

their arms to the Azzurri.

The Italians certainly made an instant impact on the tournament, beating Scotland in their first-ever outing as a fully fledged Six Nations side.

The Scots demanded Italy's expulsion on the grounds they weren't actually meant to win any games, but the organisers reasoned they'd rather have a pizza and a nice Chianti than a haggis and a pint of heavy any day and told them where to go.

Taffy Kiwis' passport woe
Adopted All Blacks exposed

Welsh rugby was plunged into an embarrassing crisis in 2000 when it emerged that New Zealand-born players Shane Howarth and Brett Sinkinson were not actually qualified to play for Wales.

The Kiwi duo had told officials they had Welsh grandparents, which according to the rules meant they could play for the Principality. But rather than bothering to actually check their credentials, the desperate WRU had simply rolled out the welcome mat, politely tried to ignore their accents and hastily handed them the lyrics to the national anthem.

The red faces of the WRU officials matched the red of the team's jersey and both adopted Taffys were quickly, but not so quietly, dropped from the team.

Instant replay
Rugger gets new video gizmo

Rugby entered a new technological era in 2000 with the first use of video replay technology to rule whether a try had been scored and, sadly, put an end to many a drink-fuelled, post-match argument.

Of course, it took the International Rugby Board time to find a referee who could actually operate a video recorder (they're not really the brightest bunch, are they?) but, once that little problem had been ironed out, it was full steam (or should that be fast forward?) ahead.

The first time a video referee was called into action was during New Zealand's clash with Tonga in June when Englishman Steve Lander asked for help from his fourth official on a disputed "try" by All Black forward Todd Blackadder. The score was awarded and rugby fans everywhere would soon learn to love the sight of out-of-breath referees making that square sign with their fingers to indicate a replay was needed. Because they hadn't kept up with the play. And were knackered. And too scared to actually make a decision themselves.

104 Jonny too good

The pupil becomes the master

Jonny Wilkinson has already broken more records during his international career than a butter-fingered DJ having a really bad day. The Newcastle and England No.10 with the deadly left boot just can't seem to stop scoring (or getting injured, of course).

One of his first major milestones came in 2001 when he became England's all-time leading scorer. England thumped France 48–19 at Twickenham and Saint Wilko became the first Englishman to pass the 400-point barrier in Tests, surpassing the previous best of Rob Andrew, his Newcastle coach and mentor. It had taken Andrew 69 games to rack up his total; his protégé needed a mere 27.

Lord Wilkinson celebrated his achievement with his customary glass of orange juice, three hours of extra practice and a good rub down with sandpaper. Andrew smiled, gritted his teeth and secretly vowed to spray deep heat on Wilko's jockstrap at the next training session.

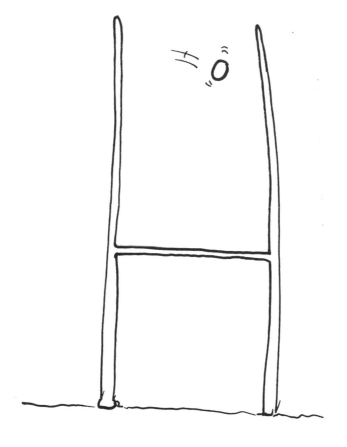

Believe it or not but the first player to score over a 1000 points in international rugby was not, in fact, Crown Prince Jonny. No, that honour actually goes to Welsh fly-half Neil Jenkins, who took his personal points tally into four figures in 2001 when Wales played England at the Millennium Stadium.

The flame-haired (okay, ginger) No.10 converted Scott Quinnell's 65th minute try to take him to 1001 points in internationals. It was the only highlight on a miserable afternoon for Wales, however, as England emerged 44–15 winners.

Jenkins was not the kind of player to get too carried away about things either way. The fly-half may have rattled up a record haul of points, but he never felt there was a whole lot of loving from the fans. "In Wales," he once said, "the half-backs, especially the stand-off, always get the blame.." Poor lad.

High five!

Try revalued to make the game more exciting

In 2002 the International Rugby Board decided it was high time to encourage more attack-minded rugby with more tries scored. They were worried the game was becoming dominated by the kickers and, since it wasn't really feasible to tie all their laces together, they increased the value of a try from four to five points.

It took a while to explain to some players (mainly the props) but they finally grasped the concept and everyone agreed it was a super wheeze.

The last-ever "four pointer" (assuming the IRB don't change their minds) was scored by Scotland prop David Sole in the same year against Australia. The first "five pointer" also came against the Wallabies in 2002 – the All Blacks' Va'aiga Tuigamala crossing for the historic score.

The name's Clive, Clive Woodward

England coach comes over all "007" in World Cup build-up

Soon-to-be-Sir Clive Woodward left nothing to chance as England prepared for the 2003 World Cup Down Under. Every detail of the team's build-up was meticulously planned, from their individual dietary requirements (pies or burgers?) to making sure they hadn't left the gas on at home.

Woody even had the team hotel swept for bugs – the electronic rather than hairy, potentially poisonous variety – before every team meeting to ensure those dastardly Aussies weren't eavesdropping on their plans.

The paranoia paid off, of course, as England cruised into the final to face Australia, who were blissfully unaware of Woodward's cunning plan to deliberately take the game into extra-time, give every England fan a heart attack and then let Jonny Wilkinson win the game 20–17 Roy of the Rovers-style with a drop goal in the dying seconds. Pure genius.

The England team were accorded a hero's welcome when they returned home, a nice trip to Buckingham Palace to meet Queenie and the free use of an open-top bus for the day. The Aussie team narrowly escaped being fed to the sharks.

108 Keeping up with the Joneses

Wales play the name game in 2005 in desperate bid to confuse Springboks

Over the years the Welsh rugby team has never exactly been short of players called Jones, Davies, Evans and Williams. In fact, any international hopeful from the Principality not bearing one of the four holy surnames has been met with suspicion and ridicule, very much in the same way any Australian not christened Bruce or Shane is usually socially ostracised and denied basic health care (and that includes the women).

So it was little surprise in 2004 when the Welsh selectors named a team to face South Africa at the Millennium Stadium with a record six (unrelated) Joneses in the starting line-up.

The Jones roll of honour for the game was Stephen (fly-half), Adam (prop), Duncan (prop), Steve (hooker), Dafydd (flanker) and Ryan (number eight) – and doubtless there were thousands of namesakes in the crowd.

And the ingenious tactic almost worked too as Wales pushed the Springboks all the way before going down 38–36. If only they'd gone the whole hog and selected Aled, Vinnie and Tom as well...

"And Jones, Jones, Jones, Jones and Jones are in support of, er, Jones…"

Char 'n' Gav go public
Waxy-legged Welsh centre and teen chanteuse get it on

Rugby got its first real taste of the "Posh 'n' Becks" factor in 2005 when it emerged Grand Slamming, leg-shaving Lion Gavin Henson and Welsh warbler Charlotte Church were, ahem, stepping out together. As well as falling out of an assortment of nightclubs.

The loved-up duo were so inseparable that little Charlotte even followed gorgeous Gavin all the way to New Zealand with the British & Irish Lions to watch him get chewed up and spat out by the All Blacks.

The comparisons between the golden couple and Mr and Mrs Beckham were inevitable. Both men were famous for their sporting prowess, good looks and metrosexual grooming habits. Ms Church, on the other hand, Is actually a very **talented** singer.

Heavyweight squad mauled
Woodward's Lions tamed by the Kiwis

It was a miracle the plane that flew the 2005 British & Irish Lions to New Zealand actually made it off the ground. With a record 45-strong playing squad, more coaches than a National Express garage, countless back-up staff and the additional weight of spin doctor Alistair Campbell and his ego, Sir Clive Woodward's party was lucky to get off the Heathrow tarmac.

Sadly, there were to be no more miracles once the plane landed

"This is your captain speaking. We are cruising at an altitude of 30 feet…"

with a bump on New Zealand's sheep-laden land. The Lions huffed and puffed, skipper Brian O'Driscoll was injured in the first minutes of the first Test, Michael Owen nipped off to change nappies back home and then flew back again, and the All Blacks recorded a ridiculously easy series whitewash.

Quite what our old friend William Webb Ellis would have made of the whole £10 million jaunt is a debate for another time...

GAME OVER